E. JACK SHARPE
P.O. BOX 156
WHITE CLOUD

PUBLIC LIBRARY
WHITE CLOUD, MICH.

Y0-EAZ-628

J 808.3 Dub

Dubrovin, Vivian.

Write your own story

DE 27 '89
JE 18 '90
JA 5 '91
FE 6 '91
JE 1 '91
MY 31 '93
OC 13 '93

E. JACK SHARPE PUBLIC LIBRARY
P.O. BOX 156, 1038 WILCOX AVE.
WHITE CLOUD, MI 49349

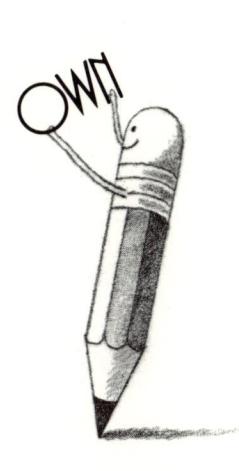

WRITE YOUR OWN STORY

WRITE YOUR OWN STORY

BY VIVIAN DUBROVIN

**Illustrations by
ANNE CANEVARI GREEN**

Franklin Watts
New York/London/Toronto/Sydney/1984
A First Book

Library of Congress Cataloging in Publication Data

Dubrovin, Vivian.
　Write your own story.

　(A First book)
　Includes index.
　Summary: Discusses some of the many ways to write a short story, explaining how to begin with an idea, create characters, plot, and dialogue, and edit the finished story.
　　1. Fiction—Authorship—Juvenile literature.
2. Short story—Juvenile literature. [1. Fiction—Authorship. 2. Short story. 3. Authorship.
4. Creative writing] I. Title.
PN3377.D83　　1984　　808.3'1　　83-23353
ISBN 0-531-04739-3

Copyright © 1984 by Vivian Dubrovin
All rights reserved
Printed in the United States of America
6　5　4　3　2　1

Chapter One
Introduction
1

Chapter Two
Where Do I Begin?
3

Chapter Three
Create a Character
11

Chapter Four
Create a Story
17

Chapter Five
Make It Exciting
27

Chapter Six
Dialogue Is Not Just Talk
31

Chapter Seven
A Title for Your Story
37

Chapter Eight
What Do You Mean, Edit?
39

Chapter Nine
Collecting Ideas
43

Chapter Ten
Reading for Ideas
49

For Further Reading   53
Index   55

To Ross and Emilie Herr
(my parents)
for their support in those early writing years

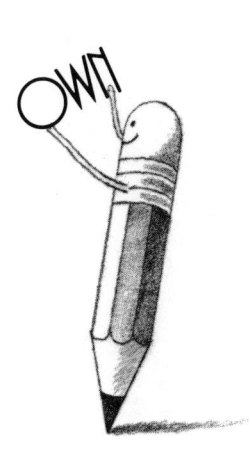

WRITE YOUR OWN STORY

1 INTRODUCTION

There are as many ways to write a story as there are kinds of stories. If you were to study all the ways and all the stories and all the parts of stories before you wrote your first one, the job would become so awesome that you probably would never pick up a pencil.

Writing a story is a lot like picking up that first handful of snow, patting it into shape, and creating a snowball. Then you begin to roll it around the yard and pick up more snow. It becomes a bigger ball and you begin to think about the snowman you are now creating.

That first snowman might be quite ordinary. But, when you walk down the street and see the snowmen your friends have made, you will collect ideas for your next one. Maybe you'll add arms, ears, and other details. Maybe it won't be a person at all, but a snow creature. Maybe it'll be a snow fort, a snow car, a spaceship, or a snow castle.

Some people become so carried away with creating snow sculptures that they dash outside when only a few snowflakes fall just to create the tiniest model. They create from the snow in their backyard, snow in the school yard, and snow in the park. They will go anywhere they can find some of that special stuff.

Then, one day, a blizzard dumps two feet of endless snow to create all the ideas they've collected.

Writing stories is like that.

This book is intended to help you pick up that first handful of ideas, shape them, and create that first story.

2
WHERE DO I BEGIN?

Want to write a story? Your very own story?

Reading is fun. A good book can take you on an exciting adventure. Writing can also be an exciting adventure.

How do you begin?

You can begin in any of many different ways. Sometimes a character suggests a story. An old man with bushy white hair and a beard that almost covers his face struggles with a cane while trying to board your school bus. You know it's Jimmy's grandfather coming to talk to Jimmy's class today, but he sure looks a lot like Santa Claus. What would it be like if Santa Claus really got on your bus one day?

Sometimes it's a place that sparks an idea. You walk home from school past a broken-down shed or a yard with three big dogs and a very low fence. You visit Aunt Zelda by getting on an elevator that goes up twenty-three floors.

Sometimes it's something that happens. You come home and find your dog is lost. There is a fight in the school yard between two of your best friends and both want your help. Or you're the first one at the scene of an auto accident.

A person, a place, something that happens, but more than that. A special something, a magic something. Can you find the magic word in each of these examples? That magic word is the real place where stories begin. That magic word is *you*.

You are on the bus. *You* visit Aunt Zelda. *You* are caught between two friends who are fighting.

The Number 1 rule of writing is to write about something you know. Why? It's the magic that makes your story seem real.

If you write about playing football and you've never played the game, you may make a mistake about some of the rules or how it feels to be tackled. Someone who plays football will recognize these mistakes and not believe your story.

But, you say, nothing exciting ever happens to you! And, besides, you'd rather write science fiction or fantasy.

Nothing exciting ever happened to Bob. He came home from school every day and watched TV. An hour later his big brother came home and switched channels. One day Bob got mad.

"You always watch your program. I want to watch mine."

"Your program is dumb," his big brother said. "Besides, I have to watch mine for school." He turned the sound up louder.

Bob went to his room. He turned on the radio as loud as it would go.

The next day Bob's teacher asked him to write a story. Bob wrote about two boys on a spaceship from another galaxy. They were watching the video screen of a planet monitor as they traveled through space. The younger brother had the screen focused on Earth, but his big brother came into the room and turned it to Venus.

The younger brother yelled, "You always watch Venus. I want to watch Earth!" He grabbed a cassette of Earth songs and turned it up as loud as he could.

Or maybe something like this happened to you.

Lisa liked to write fantasy stories about castles and a prince or princess. She also liked to ride her horse, Starburst. The old mare was well trained and gentle, and Lisa could put just a halter on her and ride around the pasture.

One day as Lisa came to the gate, her mother called from the kitchen, "You can use that halter in the pasture, but if you go out on the road, put a bridle on Starburst."

Lisa thought that was silly. Starburst responded to leg cues and never spooked at cars. Why should Lisa use a bridle?

When Lisa wrote her next fantasy story, the princess leaped on a winged Pegasus.

"Put a bridle on," called the queen from the castle.

"A bridle on Pegasus? Ridiculous!" said the princess. She flew away. "I can *talk* to Pegasus. Why should I use a bridle?"

The most successful writers are those who can turn the ordinary things in their lives into exciting adventures on paper.

What ordinary things happen to you that could be bits and pieces in your stories?

Let's find out. Let's take an imaginary treasure hunt to collect some "ordinary things" to use later. You'll need a *big* treasure bag.

Treasure Hunt List

Treasures from Home   Where do you live? A ranch? A city apartment?
With whom do you live? Mom? Dad? Grandma? Uncle Joe?
Do you have a room of your own? Share one with brother or sister?
What things are your very own?

Treasures from School   Where do you go to school? A big city school? A small private one?
How do you get there? Walk? Bus? Car?
What classes do you like? Why?
What classes do you dislike? Why?

Treasures from Hobbies   What do you do after school? On holidays?

What sports do you like? Running? Skating? Skiing? Tennis? Baseball?
Have you made anything? A model? A game? A puzzle?
Do you collect things? Stamps? Cards? Coins? Pictures?
Do you belong to a club? Boy Scouts? Girl Scouts? Camp Fire? YMCA? City recreation?
What things do you do in this group?

Treasures from Religion and Culture

Do you go to church?
Are there some things your family believes you should or shouldn't do? Rules to follow?
Are there some special holidays that your family celebrates? How? What do you do?

—7—

Did your parents or grandparents come from another country? Do they still do some things like they did "in the old country"?

Do some family members have special ideas? Grandma won't open an umbrella in the house. Uncle Tom pounds on a table and says, "knock on wood" when he wants good luck.

Treasures from Experiences

Have you ever seen an accident? A fire? A fight? Were you afraid?

Have you ever been given an award, a ribbon, a trophy? How did it feel? Was it a surprise?

Have you ever lost a pet or found someone else's? What did you do?

Did you ever lose your lunch? Your lunch money?
Have you ever been lost? How did it feel?
Have you had to take care of someone or something? Did you have any problems?

Treasures from Dreams

Have you ever had a bad dream? What was it? Why were you afraid?
Have you ever had a silly dream?
Are you afraid of dreams?

Treasures from Feelings and Relationships

Do you get along with your brothers and sisters or parents?
Is there someone you know who has something you wish you had?
Is there an animal, toy, or person that you love very much?

> Treasures from Feelings and Relationships (continued)
>
> Is there someone who does something you wish you could do? An older sister or brother?
> Is there someone who creates problems? A neighborhood bully? A pesty kid next door?

Nothing ever happens to you? Are you sure? You have lots of story pieces around you every day.

Put your treasure bag aside now. See how many times you reach into it as you create your story. The more times you do, the better your story will be.

3
CREATE A CHARACTER

Your story should have one main character.

Characters are the actors in your story. They can be people, animals, or creatures you make up.

But there should be just one star. Do not write about a boy and a girl going on an adventure, or a group of boys and girls getting on a boat. Tell about just one main person, animal, or made-up creature.

The one main character can take his or her best friend along on this adventure, or he or she can be with a group of friends. But it should be *his* or *her* story, told through *his* or *her* eyes.

When you tell a story this way, through the eyes of your main character, your reader will see your story through the eyes of this main character. The reader will be in your story. He or she will care what happens. He or she will want your main character to win. And your reader will like your story.

— 11 —

The more you know about your main character, the more exciting and interesting your story will be. For example, you could start a story this way:

A boy and his dog were walking down the street.

Boy? Dog? What does the boy look like? What is he thinking? Why is he walking down the street? How big is the dog? Does it walk slowly, heel obediently, or bound along dragging the boy behind?

Let's try to answer some of those questions right away and get the story off to a more exciting start.

I was walking Prince down Fourth Avenue last Thursday. It was snowing lightly. He kept bounding ahead, pulling me. I told myself he was only a puppy, even though he weighs more than I do, and that he'd been in the house all day. But I knew about his special powers, and he knew what was ahead, just around the next corner.

What more do you know about your main character? What happens in the rest of your story will depend on just how well you do know your character.

When you are tempted to say, "I don't know," it is time to reach back into that treasure bag you created in Chapter 2.

Story characters are never the real people in your life. They are created from bits and pieces of many people you have met or known. A story character may have Aunt Susie's twinkly eyes or Uncle Charley's chuckly laugh. Or the character may have the same bad habit as your friend Butch who never does the things he promises. The character may have some of the hopes, dreams, or fears from your treasure bag.

Before an author writes a story, he or she often creates a character sketch. This means that the author writes down all the things he or she knows about the character.

Some boys and girls feel this is a lot of extra work. They want to get on with the story, to create the character as they go along.

You can create your character as you create your story (and your character will grow with the story anyway), but leaving too much for later will cause problems for you. Creating your character before you begin writing your story is a little like counting your money before you go to the store.

When your story character comes to a river, will he or she swim across or try to build a raft? If you already know that the character is a good swimmer, you know what he or she will do. If you are creating the character as you go along, he or she may also swim across. What if you have let the character be afraid of water earlier in the story? You will need to go back and make a lot of changes to make your story logical.

There are some things your character can learn to do in your story, but there are some skills that take a lot of practice to learn. Your character will have to *know* how to do them before your story starts.

What can he or she do? What does he or she think or want? What things are important to him or her? Let's find out. Sometimes the finding out can be as much fun as writing the story.

Read all the questions on page 14 before you begin to answer any of them. You do not need to answer them all or in any special

Character Sketch Questions

What does this character look like?
How old is the character?
Is the character happy or sad? Shy or friendly? Afraid or brave? What is he or she afraid of?
What does he or she like to do? Does he or she have a hobby?
What are his or her skills? What can or can't he or she do?
Where does he or she live?
Where does he or she like to go? Travel?
What does he or she like to eat?
Does he or she have brothers and sisters? Are they older or younger?
Does the character have one parent or two? Does he or she get along with the family or fight with them?
What does he or she think of the people he or she meets?
Does he or she like school?
Does the character have any pets? Does he or she like animals?
Is he or she lazy or full of pep?
Does he or she like to be alone or with others?
Does he or she have a sense of humor? If so, does it help the character or get him or her into trouble?

order. You may want to tell a lot about one thing and very little about another.

The best character sketches are written as a theme or composition rather than questionnaire-type answers that use only a few words. Writing a composition allows your mind to take off on an idea.

Pretend you are talking to a friend, telling that person about another friend of yours. Or, you might want to pretend that your character is telling about himself or herself.

Write down the ideas as they come into your head. Don't worry about sentences, spelling, or punctuation. Just concentrate on ideas and putting them on paper.

Give your main character a name. You might want to create a special name. Don't use the name of someone you know, or your character will tend to become that person instead of the new person you are creating.

Did some things in your character sketch seem more important than others? Most of the things you learned about your character will become part of your story. Remember that you do not need to use everything.

Let's do a little story planning now and learn how to use this character sketch to create a story.

4
CREATE A STORY

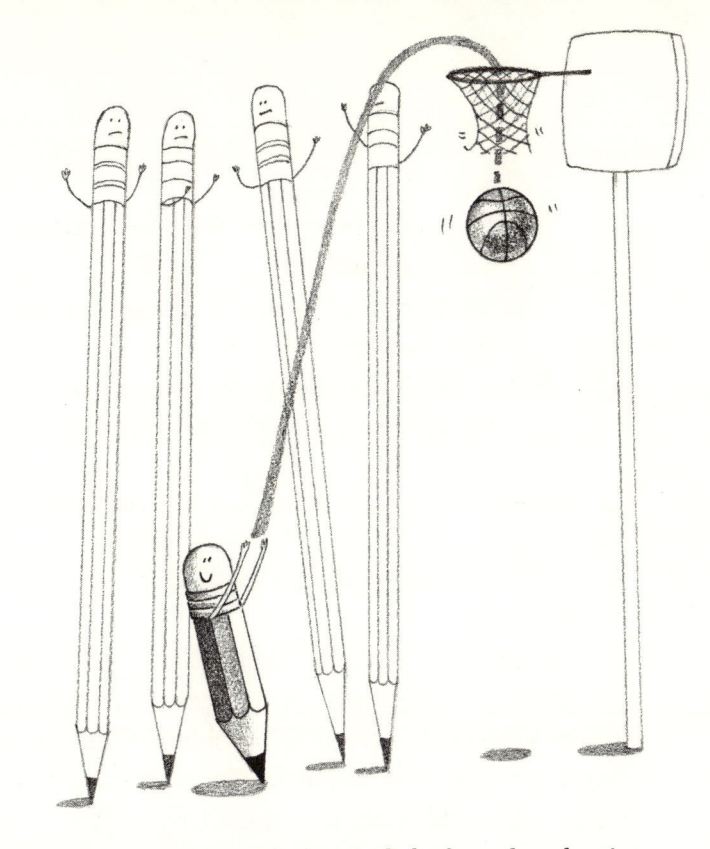

Many authors create their stories in their minds before they begin writing. They have their stories planned before they pick up their pencils or set up their typewriters.

If you can learn to do a little story planning *before* you begin writing, you can save a lot of rewriting and correcting later.

Story planning, then, is really just thinking and creating in your head before you begin writing on paper.

Begin your planning by thinking of the total story. Plan to create a short story. After you have learned the correct structure for a short story, you can write a longer one. The most important thing for you to accomplish in your first story is to learn to write a complete story. *To be complete, your story should have a beginning, a middle, and an ending.*

> The *beginning* introduces the main character and his or her problem.
> The *middle* tells what the main character does and what happens.
> The *ending* tells how the main character solves the problem and how the story ends.

A complete short story can be told in one page or up to about seven pages.

Besides being short and complete, your first story should also be simple. A simple story is basically a character with a problem and how he or she solves that problem. One easy way to describe a *simple story plan* is to put it into a formula. If you were in math class, you might write a formula this way:

$$(1 + 1) + 2 = 4$$

To turn it into a story formula, we could write it this way:

$$(\text{Character} + \text{Problem}) + \text{How Character Solves Problem} = \text{STORY}$$

You have already created a character. And from your character sketch you could probably create many stories. But, just as a simple short story must have one main character, the character must have only one problem. One problem for one story. If you think up more than one problem, you may want to write more than one story.

How do you find this problem? Problems, like the characters themselves, usually come from the experiences that you, your friends, or your relatives have had.

Look at your treasure bag in Chapter 2 and see if you can find or create some problems. Some things to look for are:

A character who *wants something*
A character who *thinks or believes something*
A *special characteristic that can produce a story* (a person who is overly kind, careless, or a show-off, etc.)

To create a problem from the things we find, we must create opposition, or conflict. Look at some possibilities from the treasure bag:

Treasures from Home

Erin wants a room of her own/but has to share one with her sister.
Jake and his brother are supposed to take the trash out/but his brother will not help.
Katie is supposed to have the table set before her mother comes home/but she lost her key and can't get into the house.

Treasures from School

The boys and girls tease Ben because he's always so early at the bus stop/but he has to leave when his mother does.

Betty copies everything Judy does/but the teacher thinks Judy is the one who is cheating.

When Les makes good grades on his report card/his best friend stops speaking to him.

Treasures from Hobbies

Dave wants to be on the basketball team/but doesn't think he's good enough.

Harley has a model car collection/but some cars keep disappearing and reappearing.

Rita's Camp Fire group is going horseback riding/but she's afraid of horses.

Treasures from Experiences

The nicest little dog follows Kristy home/but she lives in an apartment where no pets are allowed.

Kirk would like to win a ribbon or trophy/but most of his teammates can swim faster.

Do you see how it works? Can you create some story problems from your treasure bag?

Sometimes you can add a little twist to the problem. For fun, you might want to substitute animals for people and give them people problems. The monster wanted to make friends, but frightened everyone he met. The dragon didn't like to babysit and kept thinking up silly excuses. The elephant needed a birthday present for his trainer, but was too big to go into the gift shop.

You can also turn some experiences around. The ghost was afraid to go near the haunted house on Halloween. The rabbit's best friend was a hawk, but his rabbit friends wouldn't believe him.

And, as we mentioned in Chapter 2, you can change real life stories into science fiction or fantasy by changing the background.

Remember, however, that to create these stories, you must have once experienced the same *feeling*. Have you been a newcomer needing to make friends? Have you had to watch a younger brother or sister or babysit for a neighbor? Have you needed a birthday present for a friend? Have you been caught between two friends who are fighting with each other?

Look over your character sketch again.
Go through your treasure bag carefully.
Pick one problem for your story.

When you have chosen one problem, think about that problem for a little bit. You can now begin using the magic word. This one word can help make your stories special and more interesting to read. It helps you solve the problem for your character and puts meaning behind the action.

That magic word is *why!*

The more times you can ask and answer "why" in your story, the better your story will be.

Why does your character have the problem?
Why does your character want what he or she wants?
Why does your character think the way he or she thinks?
Why does your character do what he or she does?
Why does your character say what he or she says?

For example, to see how this "why" works, let's take the girl who wanted a room of her own. Let's ask Erin *why* she wants a room of her own. She might answer this way:

"Last week when I went to Clara's house, I saw her room. It's the most wonderful place. It's all her own and she can hang pictures, any pictures she wants, all over her walls."

But Erin's parents won't let her hang pictures on her wall. You will need to create a reason *why* her parents won't let her.

Erin, however, has told you in her answer that she wants a *place* of her own, not necessarily a *room*, where she can be creative and express herself. Your story will be about how she uses this same creativity to *create her own place*.

When you have finished asking all the "whys" you can think of, you will understand your character and his or her problem pretty well. You are now ready to create your story. Answering the following five questions will give you a story outline from which to work.

Story Outline Questions

1. What is your character's problem?
2. What does your character do because of this problem?
3. What happens because of what he or she does?
4. How does he or she solve the problem?
5. How does the story end?

Take a few story problems for examples and ask these questions.

1. Rita's Camp Fire group is going horseback riding, but Rita is afraid of horses.
2. Rita brings her instant camera and takes pictures of everyone else on their horses so that she won't have to get on one.
3. The other girls think this is a great idea and want Rita to have a picture, too.
4. They all help her on the horse, hold the horse, and crowd together for a group picture for Rita.
5. Rita tacks her picture on her bulletin board to prove she was brave enough to get on a horse.

1. Katie has to have the table set before her mother comes home, but she can't find her house key. Mother had wanted to leave one on the back porch, but Katie had wanted to prove she was *responsible enough* to carry one.
2. Katie hunts through the back porch, hoping Mother has hidden one anyway.
3. She finds the picnic basket still loaded with paper plates and cups from last weekend.
4. She sets the picnic table on the back porch with the paper plates and cups and napkins and plastic spoons.
5. When Katie's mother comes home, she is pleased that Katie has been *responsible enough* to set a table, and the family enjoys the picnic.

1. Lenny wants to be on the basketball team, but he is so self-conscious that when his friends start teasing him he messes up at morning tryouts.
2. Lenny runs home at lunch and gets his own ball and practices all through lunch.
3. The coach and his friends catch him practicing.
4. He knows they've seen him doing a good job, and he ignores his friends' taunts.
5. He makes the team at afternoon tryouts.

Now that you know what's going to happen in your story, you must decide where your story is going to start. Just as many TV programs begin with a dramatic scene before the first commercial, your story should also get off to an exciting start. Plan a dramatic scene to open your story and introduce the characters and the problem. This is your *beginning*, the answer to question 1 (see page 23).

The *middle* of your story will answer questions 2 and 3.

The *ending* will answer questions 4 and 5.

Be sure you have a good ending. Your character must *solve* his or her problem. And you, as the author, must figure out this solution or ending.

If you have trouble with the ending, something is probably wrong with your beginning. The ending will almost always be the opposite of the beginning. (He wanted friends when he joined the team. They lost the game, but he made a lot of friends.)

Remember to use the magic word "why" if you have trouble solving your problem.

Story problems are like puzzles. Some are harder than others. But they are not finished until the last piece is in place.

Now your story is planned. It's growing so fast in your head that it's getting hard to remember. New ideas are beginning to pop all over the place. You are beginning to see scenes taking place.

Now you are ready to write!

5
MAKE IT EXCITING

You're ready to write your story. You have your character and his or her problem. You have your story outline. You've used your magic word "why."

You have a comfortable spot picked out (curled on your bed, under the dining room table, against a big shade tree in the backyard). It's a place where you like to write. All your pencils are sharpened. And you have a thick stack of paper handy.

Now it's time for the magic trick. You've used the magic word and your story has grown in all directions. Now you can use a magic trick that will make your story exciting and seem like it's happening *right now*.

Put your character on! On Halloween you put on a costume and become—or pretend to become—the being the costume represents. When you write a story, you can do the same thing. Put your main character on, like a Halloween costume. Pretend to *be* your main character. Pretend you are in the story, at the scene, in the middle of the action. Tell the story as if it is happening right now.

Write down what is going on around you. What are people saying to you? How do you respond?

What do you see people doing? How do you feel inside? What do you do? Can you smell or taste anything? Can you describe the place where you are?

Remember your story plan. Maybe your story is all one long scene. Maybe it's several shorter scenes.

When you are pretending to be your main character, it will probably be easiest to tell your story using "I."

> I ran across the baseball field. Tim had to be here and I had to find him.
> The coach looked at me. "Sam," he said. "You can do it."

Telling your story as if you are the main character is a good way to remember to include feelings and thoughts and to remember to tell only the things "I" can see, hear, or know.

Some stories, however, in which the main character is a hero or does many very brave things may sound as if "I" is bragging a lot. Then you may want to use "he" or "she" and tell the story as if you were watching your character do, say, and think the things he or she does in your story.

Use whichever *viewpoint* is most comfortable for you. The method that seems easiest for you is the best one for your story.

Remember, though, that you cannot describe yourself as others see you while you are inside your character costume. You will have to find creative ways to show what you look like. Looking into a mirror is a worn-out method. You will have to find new and clever methods of your own.

Perhaps other characters can help:

"Blond girls are dumb," Tom said.
 Something inside me growled. I clenched my teeth and my fists.
 He turned around, looked right at me, and added, "and girls with long blond braids are twice as dumb!"

If you have trouble pretending to be your main character or imagining your scene, you may need some props. If it is summer and you are writing a ski story, you may want to put on your ski jacket to remember how cold your fingers got the last time you were skiing. You may want to pick up a bat and swing it a few times to remember how scared you were when you went to bat with the bases loaded. Many authors use these methods to help them get "into" a story.

If the story or action begins to lag, if it gets less exciting, or if you get tired, it's time to end that scene and begin another.

Try to write your entire story from beginning to end without stopping. Don't worry about spelling, the right word, punctuation, or anything else. Just like when you were writing your character sketch, the important thing now is to get everything down on paper. You can make corrections later.

6
DIALOGUE IS NOT JUST TALK

Because you created your story in dramatic scenes, and told it as if you were there taking part in the action, you needed to make your characters talk. Character talk is called dialogue.

One of the first things you can do after your story is written is to check your dialogue. Read through your story. Does the dialogue *sound* like real people talking? People do not usually talk in correct sentences. You should be able to read it aloud without stumbling over the words.

There are some rules for writing dialogue, and it is easy to put these corrections into your manuscript now. As you make the corrections, you will also learn new ways to use dialogue. You may want to add them to this first manuscript or save the ideas for later stories.

— 31 —

Each time a new character speaks, begin a new paragraph. Identify the speaker in this same paragraph. Read through your story. If someone begins to speak in the middle of a paragraph, mark it with this sign, ¶, that writers and editors use. This will remind you, when you copy your story over, to begin a new paragraph at this spot.

Commas and periods should be put inside the quotation marks. Dialogue should look like this:

"I'm going home, Bob," said Lisa.

If the dialogue is broken by other words, it is written this way:

"He promised to buy me an ice cream cone," said the girl, "to eat on the way to the park."

You don't always have to say "he said," or "she called." To add variety you can use a sentence of action to identify the speaker. Be sure to put that sentence in the same paragraph as the dialogue.

"Tim, hurry up! I'm saving a seat for you!" Jake leaned out of the bus window and waved.

In real life there is more time to talk than there is in a story. When you come into a room, you can say "Hello!" Sally can say "hello," and Bert can say "hello," and everyone else in the room can say "hello," too. But in a story there is only space enough for one "hello," or you will have two pages of *hello*'s.

Check to see if you need all the dialogue you have used. Are there too many *hello*'s or words like that? Cross out the ones that are not needed.

The words you choose for your characters to say must be part of the story. Each word must have a special job, a reason for being in the story. Here are some jobs your story talk can do:

1. *Tells about the character and shows some important characteristics* (for the main character and for some of the other characters)
    "Don't push him in! Jerry can't swim!"
    "You sure are patient. I wouldn't wait that long."
    "I can ride. I've had a horse of my own for years."
    "I promised and I won't let him down."

2. *Tells about the character's problem*
    "I can't run fast enough to play baseball."
    "What'll I do? I've lost my track shoes and my race is next."

3. *Tells about how the character feels*
    "I don't believe you."
    "You shove my brother again and I'll hit you!"
    "Don't cry, Janie. I'm sorry."
    "I'm embarrassed, Joe. We should have known."

4. *Tells about the action taking place*
    "The trail class has started and they're calling your number!"
    "Oh, no! Blackie's digging up Mom's petunias again."
    "It's not here. I've looked everywhere and I can't find it."

5. *Tells about the setting*
"The snow's coming down so hard we'll have to feel our way along this fence."
"Come on, Tom. It's too dark to fish anymore!"
"Is it always so busy and crowded here?"

6. *Tells why things are happening*
"I gave it to him for his birthday."
"Sue didn't come because she didn't have a costume."
"I don't want to go. I can't play well enough."

7. *Helps create suspense*
"I've got a creepy feeling we shouldn't go in."
"Listen! Did you hear that? It's getting closer."

Don't forget to tell *how* your character is talking. You can also mention any other characteristics of the person's voice.

"Help!" she screamed from the deep end of the pool.
"Don't," Karl whispered softly. "You'll scare it."
Ben stumbled over the words. "I didn't mean to break it."

Dialogue can also provide a dramatic opening for your first scene.

> "We can't stop at the Space Station, Sam!" Warren's voice was anxious. "This transport's designed to bypass that old station. You know the problems they're having there."
>
> Sam replied calmly. "She's dying and there's no one on board who can save her."

A play is written all in dialogue. Most TV programs and movies use only dialogue and action.

The more dialogue you use, the faster paced and more dramatic your story will be. Narration (the telling part of your story) supplies the meaning and understanding but also slows the pace of the story. Try to achieve a good balance of dialogue and narration in your story.

7
A TITLE FOR YOUR STORY

The title of your story should tell what the story is about and make your reader want to read it.

Just as a good joke doesn't give away the punch line before the ending, your title shouldn't give away any secrets in your story. Your title should give some clue as to what type of story you have written. Is it a sports story? A mystery? Suspense? Or an exciting adventure?

If your story is about some sport, that sport should be mentioned in the title. What would "The Ski Race" be about?

If your story is a mystery or suspense story, the title should tell the reader that. You can use the word "Mystery" or "Secret" in the title, such as "The Mystery of the Empty Clubhouse" or "The Secret of Shady Lake."

You can also use the word "Adventure" in the title of your adventure stories, such as "The Adventures of Super Dog."

Check titles in the library. Check titles in the magazines you read. Make a long list of titles. Then pick the ones you'd like to read. What made you pick the ones you did? If you found your title in a long list, would you choose to read that story?

Here are some make-believe titles. Which ones would make you want to read the story? Why?

> Treasure Hunt in Space
> The Dragon and the Witch Queen
> The Ice Cream Monster
> Super Machine
> The Dream That Came True
> The Nightmare That Happened
> The School Bus Bully
> Macho Mouse
> Mystery of the Missing Models
> The Friendly Dinosaur
> PeeWee Tells a Story
> The Mystery of the White Horse
> The Movie from Earth

Some titles pop into your head almost as soon as the story idea itself. Others come as you are writing the story. But some titles take a lot of hard work after the story is written.

Remember that your title is an ad that is selling your story. Take time to create a good one.

8
WHAT DO YOU MEAN, EDIT?

Editing your manuscript means looking it over very carefully to be sure that you have done all the things you want to do.

After you have written your story and before you start to edit, put your manuscript aside for a few days. Let it cool.

When you first finish a story, you feel that you have written the most wonderful thing in the world. You could not change a single word. It is very hard to edit a manuscript you have just finished.

After a few days, maybe a week, you will be able to look at your story more objectively, to read it as your reader would. This is the time to make changes and improvements.

Here are some things you can look for when you *edit* your manuscript.

1. *Does your story start at the most exciting beginning place?* Sometimes authors write paragraphs or pages before the story gets exciting. Some authors throw away the first few chapters in order to find the best place for the story to begin. Don't be afraid to throw away parts of your story. Ask yourself, "Is this really needed?" Be sure that all the things introduced in the beginning of the story are used in the story. If the princess had three wishes and used only one, how many does your story really need?

2. *Is there one complete story with a beginning, a middle, and an ending?*

3. *Is it logical?* Does one thing follow another in a logical order? Are brave characters acting bravely? Are your characters doing things the way people really do them?

4. *Have you explained why things are happening?* Remember, you can't run along with your story to explain the reasons to your reader. Everything must be in your story. Have you included all the explanations?

5. *Are all the facts correct?* Check the rules of a game

such as basketball or find the price of something such as a book. Dates and times must be accurate.

6. *Does your dialogue sound real?* Read your dialogue aloud. Does it read smoothly? Does it sound like people talking? Cross out dialogue that is not needed.

7. *Is your description consistent?* If one character is a big man on the first page, he can't fit through a narrow doorway on the last page. If the house is green in the beginning, make sure it is green throughout the story.

8. *Is your ending strong?* Does your story stop at the most dramatic point, or do you take too long explaining the ending? Have you really solved your main character's problem?

9. *Is your spelling and punctuation correct?* The last bit of polish for your story is to be sure all the commas, periods, and quotation marks are where they should be. Now is the time to check the spelling and search for the right word. When you are writing, if you are not sure you are spelling a word correctly, put a circle around it. This makes it easy to find these words when you are editing.

Sometimes someone else can help you edit your story. A teacher or parent may read your story and make suggestions. Sometimes a friend or classmate can point out some improvements.

You may or may not like the suggestions they make. Sometimes some people may not understand what you are trying to say. Can you change it and make it clearer?

Learning to accept or reject criticism of your stories is often as hard as learning to write the stories themselves. Learn to look for constructive or helpful criticism. Your mother, father, or teacher can give suggestions on how the adults in your story might react in a given situation. If your uncle is a paramedic, for example, he might have some ideas for your accident scene.

Some criticism is not helpful. You will soon learn to recognize the useful comments and ignore the others.

Remember, *you* must be the final judge of the corrections and changes in your story. If it is to be your own story, *you* must be happy with it.

Now, have you made all the changes you want? Are you happy with your story? Then it is time to prepare the final copy carefully. You may want to write it in ink or type it on a typewriter.

Are you finished? Maybe.

A funny thing can happen now. Writing stories does not have a beginning, a middle, and an ending like the story itself. It's more like a circle. When you come to the end of one story, you often find an idea for another story, and it all starts over again.

Each story you write will be a little better than the one before, because—like your main character—you grow a little, and learn a little each time you write one.

9
COLLECTING IDEAS

A very magical something happens after you write your first story. You open a new door. You become a different person.

The old you still enjoys books, short stories, TV, and movies. But a new you sees things that the old you never noticed before. You may be reading or in the middle of watching a TV program or movie and suddenly think, "I could do that! I could put something like that in my next story."

Now you can begin collecting treasures in a new and bigger treasure bag. You can expand some old ideas and add some new story parts.

EXPANDING OLD IDEAS

1. *Your Idea Box*

Ideas for stories never come one at a time so that you can write one story after another. They come in bunches, a lot of ideas at one time followed by a period of no ideas at all. The empty periods worry many writers, but too many ideas can be as big a problem as no ideas at all. How do you store ideas to use later? How do you sort out or pick one idea when several of them seem good to you?

Every author has his or her own system, and you will have to find one that works for you. Every system, however, involves making notes or filing ideas. Some authors keep a little notebook in which they write ideas. Some notebooks are well organized. Some are not. Other authors keep a file of idea cards. Some authors just have a junk drawer where they throw notes until they have time to sort them.

Just a few words, a phrase, or a sentence can remind you of the idea later. Capture as many ideas as you can and store them away for the empty times. Be careful not to spend so much time on your notes that you don't have time to write stories.

2. *Your Beginnings and Endings*

Watch for the way TV programs start. What is the first scene of a movie? Did the opening capture your attention? Did it make you want to watch the rest?

How does a book begin? Some books are slow to start. There are many chapters before the action begins to get exciting. Do you like that?

A dramatic ending can leave you thinking about a story for a long time afterward. The ending must wind up the story and the last sentence can often carry more punch than the first one. Be on the lookout for good endings.

3. *Your Character Collection*

The most valuable treasures to collect for your new treasure bag are the interesting characters you meet in stories, in movies, and in real life.

You may want to make notes about these characters and include descriptions and special characteristics, habits, strange ideas, and beliefs.

Collect words that describe characteristics. Can you create characters that have these habits? Here are some to start with:

careful	loving
careless	loyal
cruel	resentful
disappointed	self-conscious
dishonest	show-off
forgiving	smug
generous	stingy
helpful	sulky
know-it-all	superstitious
lonely	suspicious

4. *Conflict and Crisis*

You created a problem in your first story by creating opposition. Perhaps your character wanted something and couldn't have it. There are many ways to create a conflict that in turn creates a crisis. Learn to look for conflict in the stories you read.

Time can create a problem. Your character may need to find or do something before a certain time. Why?

Weather is another good way to create a crisis. A storm—snow, tornado, or hurricane—is coming in. Some action needs to take place before it comes.

Try using a different method in each story you write. Using the same method again and again becomes a crutch that the writer depends upon rather than using his or her imagination. One such crutch is violence—the car chase, racing across rooftops, the shoot-out in the warehouse, the fist fight. Is it really needed? Can you find a more imaginative solution?

Remember our first rule of writing, however. Use something *you know about*. Have you ever handled a gun? Seen anyone die? Been lost in a snowstorm or caught in a hurricane? Seeing it on television or reading about it is secondhand material. To be your own story, it must come from your own experience.

ADDING NEW STORY PARTS

1. *Dramatic Climax*

Some TV programs, movies, novels, and short stories build a suspense or interest from the beginning to a point near the end where everything seems to explode or something happens to change everything. This explosion, changing, or high point of the story is called a *climax*. Look for the climax in the stories you read or watch. Plan for a climax in a story you write.

2. Theme

The theme of the story is the idea that it conveys. What is the author trying to say? What idea is he or she trying to get across? A story is often an illustration of an abstract thought. To find a theme, try telling the story in one single sentence. Collect these one-sentence themes and use them to create new stories later. An example of a theme found in many children's stories is, "If you try hard, you can win."

In your first story you started with a character and created a story. It is also possible, although much harder, to start with a story and create a character to fit it. This is what happens when you try to write from theme. You might have an idea such as "the help you give to others comes back to you when you need it most." You would then create characters and situations that would prove your theory.

3. Point of View

In your first story you told everything through the eyes of the main character. Again, this is an easy way to write your first story and the best way to get reader identification. You have probably read stories that have been told by other characters, perhaps a best friend.

There is always a good reason for choosing the storyteller. Perhaps the main character is going to do some mean things and you want someone the reader can like to tell the story. Maybe it is a mystery and you want to have some clues hidden from the reader. In the stories you read and watch, see if you can guess why other storytellers are sometimes used.

4. Experimenting with Tense

You can start a story with an exciting scene happening right now. Then you can go back to a past time to explain why things are happening or how the story began. You can bring the story back into the present to end it. Do not change tense too often in your story or it will become confusing for your reader to follow. Be sure you have kept a logical progression of events.

5. Pictures

If you like to draw, you may want to add pictures to your story. You may want to add just a few, or you may want to create a picture book. Perhaps you might want to combine the pictures and story into a comic book. You might want to read some picture books or comic books to see how closely you have copied this type of writing.

SHARING YOUR WRITING

There are many ways of sharing your writing. You may want to form a club with other writers and read your stories to one another. You may want to print your story in a school magazine or other publication.

You may want to create your own book and design your own cover. You may then keep it for yourself or use it as a gift for your mother, father, grandparent, or other relative or friend for a birthday or other special holiday. You may want to turn it into a play to be performed on a stage.

10
READING FOR IDEAS

Short stories! Simple stories! Stories about boys and girls with problems!

One of the best ways to get ideas for the stories you want to write is to read stories. If you want to write horse stories, read five or six horse stories. If you want to write mysteries, read some mystery stories. Most important, if you want to write *short stories*, be sure to read some *short stories*.

Novels have a lot of pages in which the story can develop slowly. Characters can talk a lot, and there can be plenty of scenes. But in short stories there are some shortcuts. The best way to discover these shortcuts is to read short stories.

Where can you find short stories? There are many places.

1. *Short Story Collections.* If you are interested in a special subject, such as horses, science fiction, or fantasy you can find story collections (a book with lots of short stories in it) on one subject. Check your library card catalog or ask your librarian to help you.

2. *Magazines.* Children's magazines, such as *Highlights for Children, Cricket,* or *Boys' Life* will have short stories that you will enjoy reading. Your library will have some of these. You can look through copies of them until you find some stories you would like to read.

3. *Religious Magazines and Take-home Papers.* Many of the materials you bring home from church school have stories in them, and these are usually very good problem stories. If you do not have any at your church, perhaps some of your friends will lend you some of theirs.

4. *Picture Books and Easy-to-Read Books.* Picture books and Easy-to-Read books are a very good source of short stories. Most libraries will have a good supply of these books. This is an easy-reading way to study a lot of *short* and *complete* stories.

Read the stories for fun. When you have finished, see if you can identify some of the story parts.

1. Who is the main character?
2. What is the main character's problem?
3. How are the main character and his or her problem introduced?
4. How does the main character solve his or her problem?
5. Can you find the beginning, the middle, and the ending?
6. What are the real-life scenes, if any?
7. Can you tell why the characters acted as they did?
8. How was dialogue used?
9. What is the theme? What is the author trying to say?
10. Can you tell the story in one sentence?

Reading is the best writing teacher in the world. The more you read, the more ideas you will get. The more different kinds of stories you read, the more different kinds of stories you will learn to create.

FOR FURTHER READING

Carlson, Bernice Wells. *Let's Pretend It Happened to You.* Nashville, Tenn.: Abingdon Press, 1973.

Cosman, Anna. *How to Read and Write Poetry.* New York: Franklin Watts, 1979.

P.S. Write Soon! Produced by the United States Postal Service in cooperation with the National Council of Teachers of English, 1111 Kenyon Road, Urbana, Illinois 61801.

INDEX

Accuracy, 40–41
Action, 29, 33
Adventure stories, 37

Beginning of story, 17, 25, 40, 44–45
Boys' Life, 50

Character, 3, 45
    character sketch, 13–15
    main character, 11–12, 18
    pretending to become, 28–29
Character sketch, 13–15
Climax, 46
Conflict and crisis, 19, 45–46
Consistency, 41

Corrections, 29
Cricket, 50
Criticism, 42
Culture, 7–8

Dialogue:
    and narration, 35
    rules for writing, 32–35, 41
Dreams, 9

Easy-to-read books, 50
Editing, 39
    and criticism, 42
    rules for, 40–41
Ending of story, 17, 25, 40, 41, 44–45

Excitement, how to create, 27–29, 40
Experiences, 8, 20

Fantasy, 4–5, 21
Feelings, 9–10, 21, 33

"He," 28
Highlights for Children, 50
Hobbies, 6–7, 20
Home, 6, 19

"I," 28
Ideas, 43
    beginnings and endings, 44–45
    character collection, 45
    conflict and crisis, 45–46
    idea box, 44
    new story parts, 46–48
    reading for, 49–51
Imagination, 28–29

Library, 50

Magazines, 50
Main character, 11–12
Manuscript, 39
Middle of story, 17, 25, 40

Mysteries, 37

Narration, 35
Novels, 49

Objectivity, 39

Paragraph sign, 32
Picture books, 50
Pictures, 48
Place, 3
Problems, of characters, 18–19
Props, 29
Punctuation, 41

Questions, for story outline, 23–24
Quotation marks, 32

Reading for ideas, 49–51
Relationships, 9–10
Religion, 7–8, 50
Religious magazines, 50

School, 6, 20
Science fiction, 4–5, 21
Setting, 34
Sharing your writing, 48
"She," 28

Short stories, 49–50
Spelling, 41
Story:
    formula for, 18
    outline for, 23–24
    planning for, 17–18
    problems for, 18–21, 25
Suspense, 34, 37

Take-home papers, 50

Tense, 48
Theme, 47
Titles, 37–38
Treasure hunt list, 6–10

Viewpoint, 29, 47

"Why," 22
Writing, first rule of, 4, 46

ABOUT THE AUTHOR

Vivian Dubrovin has been writing for as long as she can remember. She wrote stories for her dolls, stories for her classmates, and stories for her friends in the neighborhood. She also wrote plays and pageants that were performed on school stages and in backyards.

More recent achievements include stories for multi-media educational reading programs, and stories and articles for children's magazines. She has also directed regional workshops on writing for children and has served as a consultant for many school and individual writing projects.

A resident of Longmont, Colorado, Ms. Dubrovin is the mother of five children.